DRAW

STAR WARS®

THE CLONE WARS™

KLUTZ®

BY THE EDITORS OF KLUTZ
AND BONNIE BURTON

KLUTZ®

creates activity books and other great stuff for kids ages 3 to 103. We began our corporate life in 1977 in a garage we shared with a Chevrolet Impala. Although we've outgrown that first office, Klutz galactic headquarters remains in Palo Alto, California, and we're still staffed entirely by real human beings. For those of you who collect mission statements, here's ours:

CREATE WONDERFUL THINGS   ///   BE GOOD   ///   HAVE FUN!

LUCASFILM
Executive Editor: Jonathan W. Rinzler
Art Director: Troy Alders
Keeper of the Holocron: Leland Chee

Published by Klutz, a subsidiary of Scholastic Inc. Scholastic and associated logos are trademarks and/or registered trademarks of Scholastic Inc. Klutz and associated logos are trademarks and/or registered trademarks of Klutz.

Distributed in the UK by
Scholastic UK Ltd
Westfield Road
Southam, Warwickshire
England CV47 0RA

Distributed in Australia by
Scholastic Australia Ltd
PO Box 579
Gosford, NSW
Australia 2250

Distributed in Canada by
Scholastic Canada Ltd
604 King Street West
Toronto, Ontario
Canada M5V 1E1

Book printed in China. All components manufactured in China, 73

ISBN 978-1-59174-698-0

4 1 5 8 5 7

VISIT OUR WEBSITE
You can check out all the stuff we make, find a nearby retailer, request a catalog, sign up for a newsletter, e-mail us, or just goof off! www.klutz.com
www.starwars.com

WRITE US
We would love to hear your comments regarding this or any of our books. We have many!

KLUTZ®

450 Lambert Avenue
Palo Alto, CA 94306

WHAT'S IN HERE?

FEAR NOT!

BEFORE

SO YOU WANT TO DRAW
STAR WARS®: THE CLONE WARS™,
BUT YOUR DRAWINGS LOOK MORE LIKE
KAADU SCRATCHES...

...INSTEAD OF
PORTRAITS WORTHY OF A
MASTER JEDI.

Don't worry! You've come to the
right place. This book is full of handy
tips and pointers (just like Yoda).

AFTER

SOON A BETTER
ARTIST, YOU WILL BE!

THE PENCIL

Just as a Jedi channels his power through a lightsaber, the artist channels his or her power through a pencil. This tool enables you to work light and fast.

THE MARKER

Once you've created a pencil sketch you like, make it final with a clean black line.

COLOR

We've provided colored pencils. They are great for drawing metal droids or glowing lasers. We've given you six colors, but the galaxy is a colorful place. You may need to grab more color from your own supply.

WHOOPS!
BLOCK ERASER

THE ERASER

You're learning.
Mistakes happen.

REMEMBER, YOU ARE SUPPOSED TO DRAW IN THIS BOOK! DON'T JUST READ IT—MAKE IT YOURS!

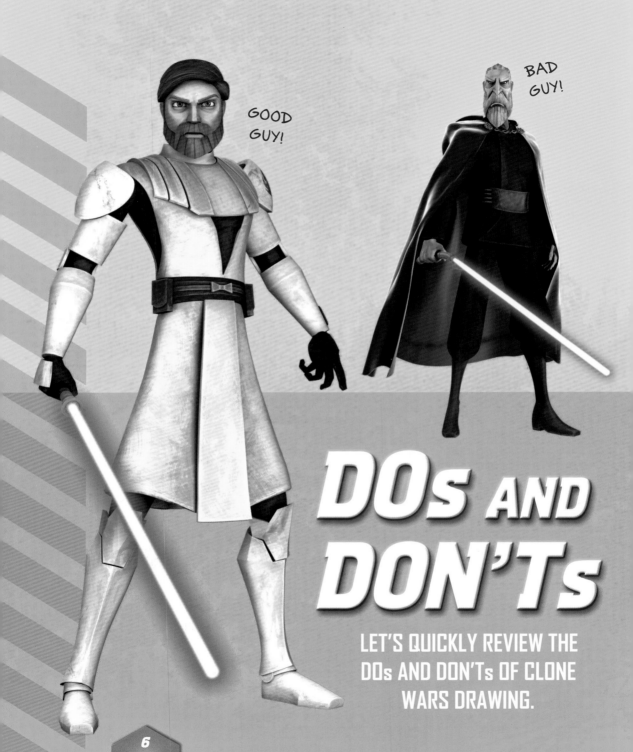

GOOD GUY!

BAD GUY!

DOs AND DON'Ts

LET'S QUICKLY REVIEW THE DOs AND DON'Ts OF CLONE WARS DRAWING.

DO work from the inside out.

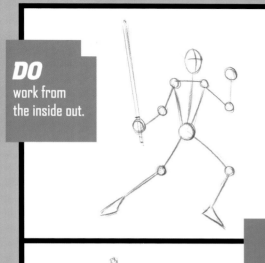

DON'T start with the outside details.

DO use your eraser.

WHOOPS! BLOCK ERASER

DO work loose, fast, and even messy.

DON'T work tiny and dark.

DO sit back from the page and relax.

DON'T hunch over your drawing.

TRACING TIME

NOW'S THE TIME TO TRACE!

Even though it's
not drawing,
tracing teaches
you about curves,
lines, and shapes.
The more you trace your
favorite characters, the more
you'll figure out the relative sizes
of their heads, legs, arms, hands, and feet,
and exactly where they should go.

GET OUT YOUR LIGHTSABER PENCIL AND START TRACING JEDI
OBI-WAN KENOBI ON THE OPPOSITE PAGE. Draw lightly and
erase lines you don't want. When you like your drawing, darken
your lines with a marker and add some color. Don't worry if the
tracing isn't perfect — that comes with practice!

OVERLINES

DRAWING JEDI, SITH, CLONES, AND DROIDS THE WRONG WAY CAN MAKE THEM LOOK LIFELESS, FLAT, AND BORING.

Here's a handy tip! Round out your drawing with "overlines," lines that cross over each other.

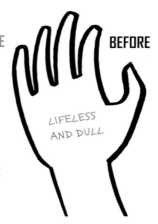

BEFORE

LIFELESS AND DULL

AFTER

OVERLINES: *LET THE LINES CROSS OVER.*

GO FROM FLAT GUY...

TO JEDI.

12

NOW IT'S YOUR TURN.

Use your pencil to add overlines and
give life to these **"flat guys."**

CHOOSE YOUR LINE
TRACING

ON THE FOLLOWING PAGES ARE A FEW CHARACTER SKETCHES.
You'll notice that all the lines are loose and, in some places, even a little messy. A real artist starts rough and then picks lines to create a more finished drawing.

DRAW DIRECTLY ON TOP OF THE BLUE LINES OF THE SKETCH. CHOOSE THE LINES YOU WANT TO TRACE. NO NEED TO TRACE THEM ALL.

PADMÉ AMIDALA

Headstrong and beautiful, Senator Padmé Amidala not only has the respect of her fellow politicians, but also the love of Jedi Anakin Skywalker.

CHANCELLOR PALPATINE

As the leader of the Galactic Senate, Palpatine's quest for ultimate power cannot be satisfied through democracy. His secret identity as Darth Sidious makes him a devious enemy of the Republic.

ANOTHER ROUGH SKETCH. Use your pencil and draw right in the book to tighten it into a final sketch.

MORE
CHOOSE YOUR LINE
TRACING

JUST LIKE BEFORE, use your pencil and turn this rough sketch into a final, tracing just the lines that look right.

PLO KOON

With his face hidden behind a forked face mask, Jedi Master Plo Koon fights alongside his fellow Jedi during the Clone Wars.

JABBA THE HUTT

The giant slug-like gangster Jabba the Hutt is notorious for his illegal activities from spice-smuggling to weapons dealing.

REMEMBER, TRACE ONLY THE MOST IMPORTANT LINES. STAY LOOSE.

STICK FIGURES

IT'S WHAT'S INSIDE THAT COUNTS.

You want to draw Jar Jar Binks.
But where to begin? The ears? The feet?
The answer is inside.

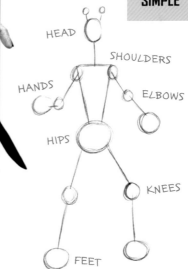

START
SIMPLE

HEAD

SHOULDERS

HANDS

ELBOWS

HIPS

KNEES

FEET

STICK FIGURE PRACTICE

EVERY GREAT DRAWING STARTS WITH A STICK FIGURE. Pros sketch light, fast, and loose with their pencils. Use these next few pages to test-drive your stick-figure skills.

MACE WINDU

As a respected Jedi Master and General, Mace Windu always weighs the options first, particularly before leading clone troopers and Twi'lek freedom fighters into battle against Wat Tambor and his Separatist forces.

DRAW CIRCLES FOR THE MAJOR JOINTS, THEN CONNECT THEM.

HEAD

SHOULDERS

ELBOWS

HANDS

HIPS

KNEES

FEET

TRACE THIS
STICK FIGURE.
STAY LOOSE!

Now do
DOOKU.

————————— HEAD —————————

————————— SHOULDERS —————————

————————— HANDS —————————

————————— HIPS —————————

————————— KNEES —————————

————————— FEET —————————

We've provided the head, you do the rest.

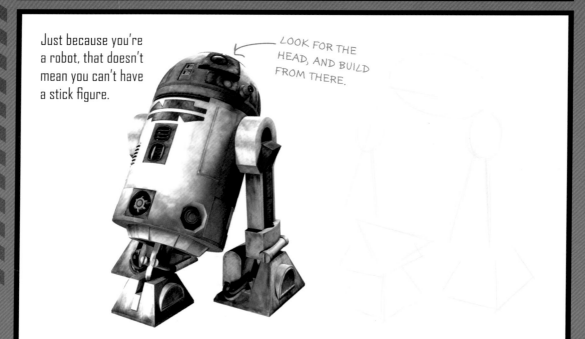

Just because you're a robot, that doesn't mean you can't have a stick figure.

LOOK FOR THE HEAD, AND BUILD FROM THERE.

We've provided the head,
you do the rest.

SEE IF YOU CAN DO THIS ONE ALL ON YOUR OWN.

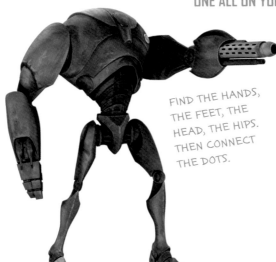

FIND THE HANDS,
THE FEET, THE
HEAD, THE HIPS.
THEN CONNECT
THE DOTS.

NOW CREATE SOME OF YOUR OWN STICK FIGURES, IN THEIR OWN POSES.

AGAIN, CREATE SOME OF YOUR OWN STICK FIGURES, IN THEIR OWN POSES.

SHAPES

THE BUILDING BLOCKS OF DRAWING

Look at Obi-Wan. A complex character, no doubt. The best way to draw him is to break him into parts, simple shapes that you add onto your stick figures.

START SIMPLE

HEAD

ARM

TRACE GENERAL GRIEVOUS ON THE OPPOSTIE PAGE.
Notice the shapes that make up his head and body.

28

SHAPE PRACTICE

ON THESE NEXT PAGES, WE'LL TAKE A CLOSER LOOK AT HEADS AND BODIES. But it's not yet time to worry about eyebrows and fingertips. Keep it simple. Circles, squares, rectangles, triangles, ovals... GO!

GET TO KNOW C-3PO.
Trace the shapes that
make his body.

C-3PO

Protocol droid C-3PO is
fluent in over six million
forms of communication,
which means he can worry in
lots of different languages.

MORE SHAPE PRACTICE

VICEROY NUTE GUNRAY IS NOT THE MOST ATTRACTIVE FELLOW. Try to look at the beauty of the shapes in his face. Not the lack of beauty in... his face.

**NOTICE THE
STICK FIGURE?**
Trace the shapes.

NUTE
GUNRAY

Cutthroat Neimoidian
Nute Gunray often abuses
his role as the Viceroy of
the Trade Federation to
bully others into signing
unfair treaties.

EVEN BIG SLOPPY CHARACTERS START WITH BASIC SHAPES.

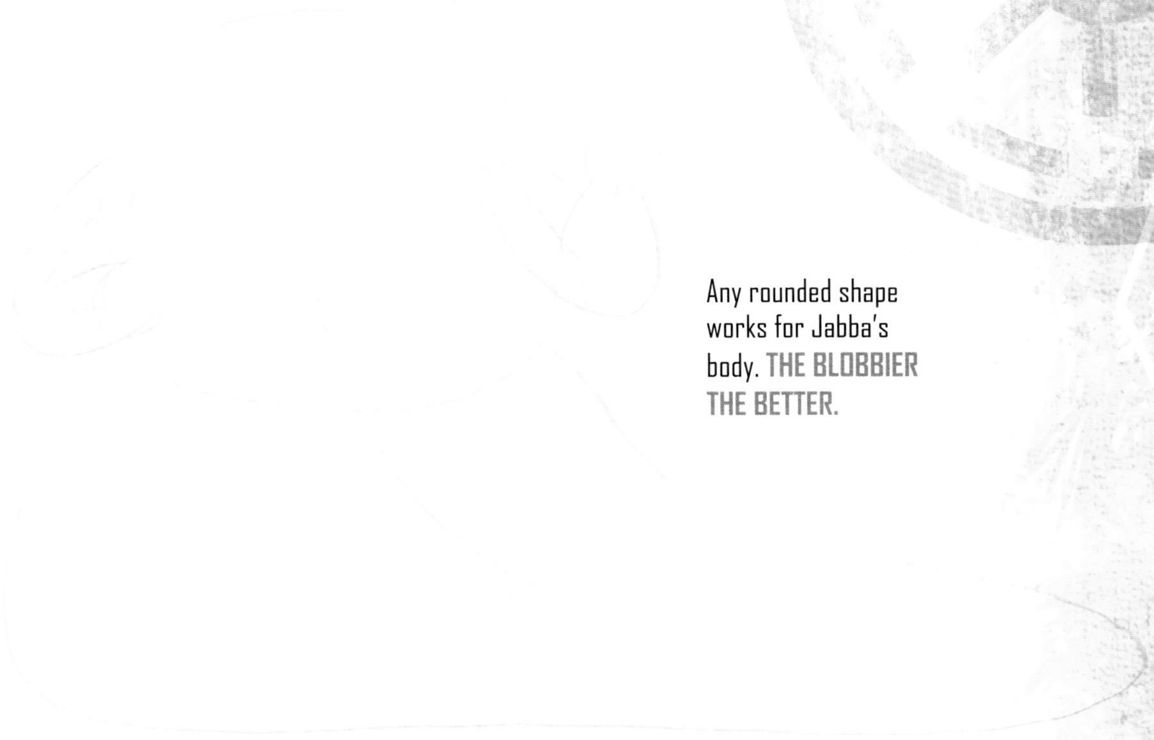

Any rounded shape
works for Jabba's
body. THE BLOBBIER
THE BETTER.

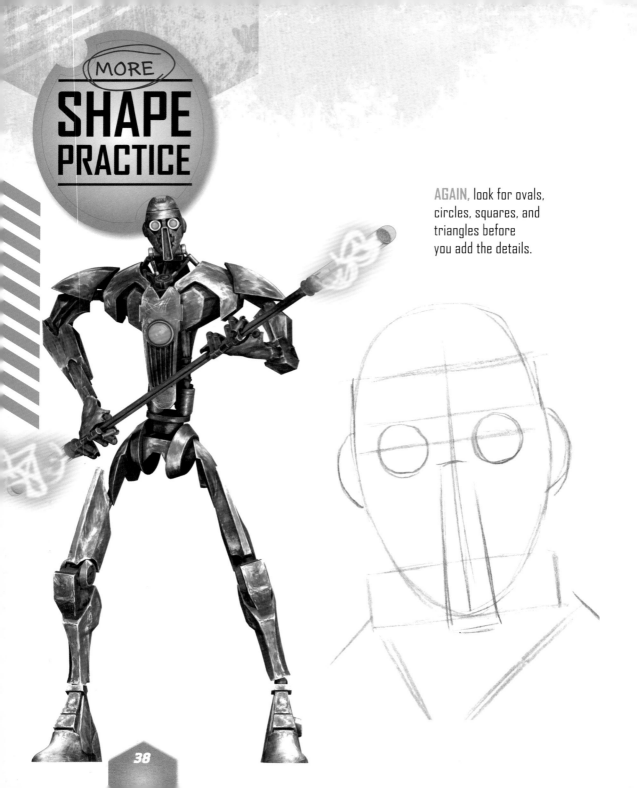

MORE
SHAPE
PRACTICE

AGAIN, look for ovals, circles, squares, and triangles before you add the details.

STAY LOOSE. STAY FAST.
DON'T WORRY ABOUT
MAKING MISTAKES.

KEEP YOUR ERASER
CLOSE BY.

IG-100 SERIES
MAGNAGUARDS
(BODYGUARD DROIDS)

General Grievous's body-
guard droids are capable of
battling multiple Jedi using
their electrostaffs that can
block lightsaber attacks.

DETAILS DETAILS DETAILS

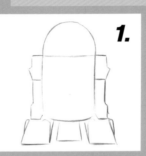 **1.**

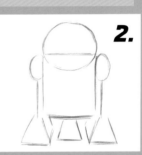 **2.**

 **3.**

 **4.**

You've drawn the stick figure. You've built up the shapes... now what?

TIME TO ADD THE DETAILS.

R2-D2

Feisty astromech droid R2-D2 always seems to save the day with his bravery, smarts, and endless gadgets.

We've provided the stick figures and the shapes of R2-D2. **TRACE THE DETAILS.**

R2-D2

Feisty astromech droid R2-D2 always seems to save the day with his bravery, smarts, and endless gadgets.

We've provided the stick figures and the shapes of R2-D2. TRACE THE DETAILS.

4 STEPS

1.
STICK FIGURE

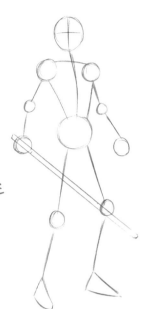

2.
SHAPES

3.
BASIC DETAILS

4.
DETAILED DETAILS

FOLLOW THE STEPS ON PAGE 44 TO DRAW ANAKIN. We've given you some lines to trace to get started.

ANAKIN SKYWALKER

Under the guidance of Master Obi-Wan Kenobi, Anakin Skywalker's skill and bravery are tested. His patience is often tested by his own young Padawan, Ahsoka Tano.

1.
STICK FIGURE

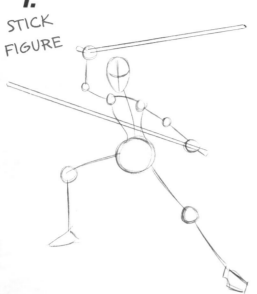

2.
SHAPES

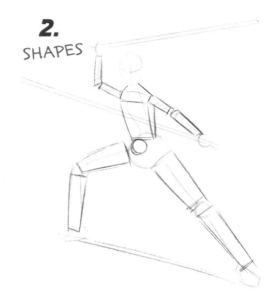

3.
BASIC DETAILS

4.
DETAILED DETAILS

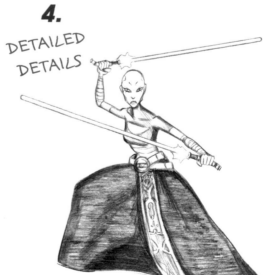

FOLLOW THE STEPS ON PAGE 46 TO DRAW ASAJJ. We've given you some lines to trace to get started.

ASAJJ VENTRESS

1. STICK FIGURE

2. SHAPES

3. BASIC DETAILS

4. DETAILED DETAILS

YODA

Jedi Master Yoda has trained Jedi for many centuries. As a General during the Clone Wars, he assigned young Padawan Ahsoka Tano to Jedi Master Anakin Skywalker.

FOLLOW THE STEPS AT LEFT TO DRAW YODA. We've given you the basic shapes.

1.

STICK
FIGURE

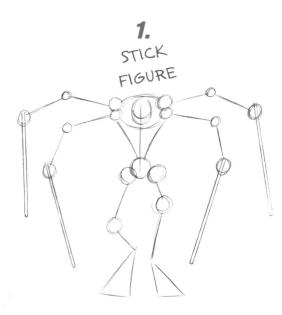

2.

SHAPES

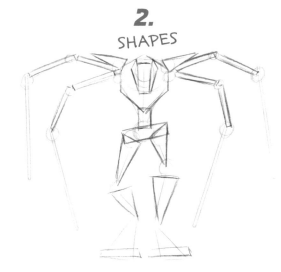

3.

BASIC
DETAILS

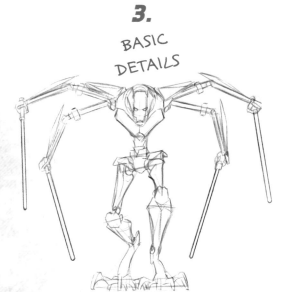

4.

DETAILED
DETAILS

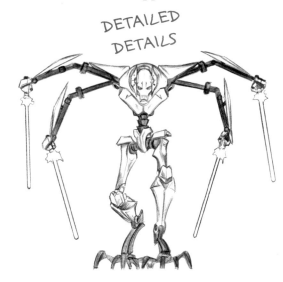

FOLLOW THE STEPS AT LEFT TO
DRAW GENERAL GRIEVOUS.
We've given you the
basic shapes.

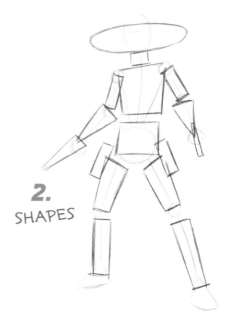

1.

STICK FIGURE

2.

SHAPES

3.

BASIC DETAILS

4.

DETAILED DETAILS

CAD BANE

**FOLLOW THE STEPS
TO DRAW CAD BANE.**
Here's the stick figure.

CAD BANE

The loyalty of galactic mercenary Cad Bane is for sale to the highest bidder. The cunning blue-skinned bounty hunter proves to be a challenging adversary for the Jedi.

1.
STICK FIGURE

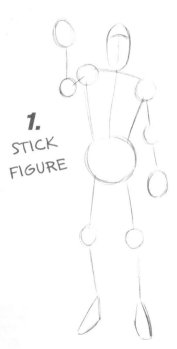

2.
SHAPES

3.
BASIC DETAILS

4.
DETAILED DETAILS

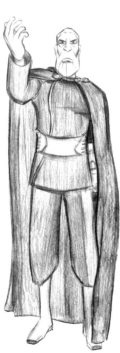

FOLLOW THE STEPS TO
DRAW COUNT DOOKU.
Here's the stick figure.

COUNT DOOKU

Under the direction of his
Master, Darth Sidious,
Count Dooku proves to be
a Sith apprentice not to
be taken lightly.

COUNT DOOKU

1.
STICK
FIGURE

2.
SHAPES

3.
BASIC
DETAILS

4.
DETAILED
DETAILS

Follow the steps to draw
Ahsoka. GOOD LUCK.

AHSOKA TANO

Appointed by Yoda to study under Anakin
Skywalker during the Clone Wars, Ahsoka, or
"Snips" as Anakin calls her, is always eager to
prove she deserves the rank of Jedi.

CLONE TROOPERS

THE GOOD GUYS

Kaminoans used DNA from bounty hunter Jango Fett to create an army of clones trained for combat. Thanks to a rapid growth-acceleration process, clones take half the amount of time to become adult troopers. They may look alike but their different personalities come in handy as they battle against the Separatists.

1.
STICK
FIGURE

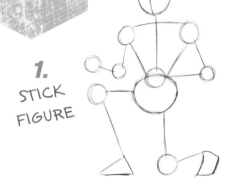

2.
SHAPES

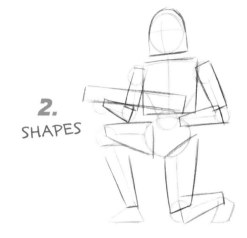

3.
BASIC
DETAILS

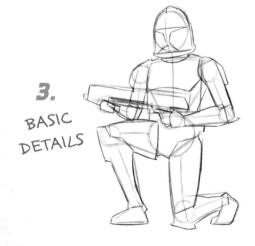

4.
DETAILED
DETAILS

FOLLOW THE STEPS TO
DRAW A CLONE TROOPER.
Here's the stick figure.

CLONE TROOPER

CLONE STYLE

HOW DO YOU TELL ONE CLONE FROM ANOTHER CLONE? THEY ARE, AFTER ALL, CLONES. Each of the clone troopers has his own haircut. Many have beards, mustaches, and tattoos. And their day jobs give them many, one-of-a-kind, battle scars.

YOUR VERY OWN CLONES

Give these look-alike soldiers unique haircuts,
facial hair, scars, and tattoos. And then
give them names, of course.

NAME: _____

NAME: _____

NAME: _____

NAME: _____

NAME: _____

NAME: _____

BATTLE DROIDS

THE BAD GUYS

While on the mindless side, the Trade Federation's army of battle droids serves its purpose with loyal mechanical soldiers that follow all orders. They are mass-produced at various droid factories on Separatist worlds and usually overwhelm their enemy with sheer numbers. These metal morons are expendable, but deadly if underestimated. Roger, roger!

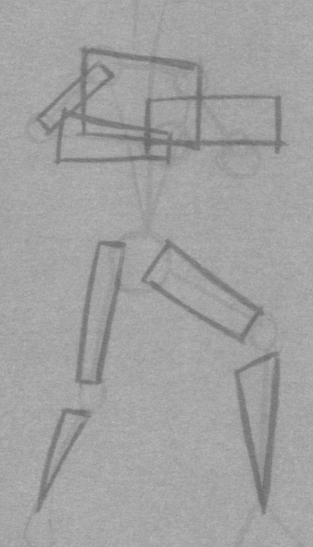

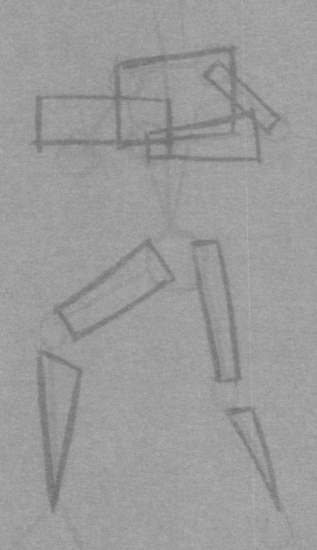

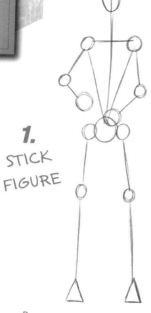

1.
STICK
FIGURE

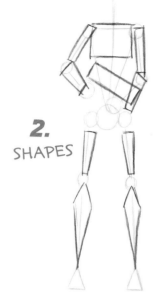

2.
SHAPES

3.
BASIC
DETAILS

4.
DETAILED
DETAILS

FOLLOW THE STEPS TO
DRAW A BATTLE DROID.
Here's the stick figure.

BATTLE DROID

EVEN THOUGH A MINDLESS SOLDIER IS A LOYAL SOLDIER, BATTLE DROIDS HAVE THEIR FLAWS AND LIMITATIONS.

AFTER THE BATTLE

WATCH YOUR BACK!

Their flimsy armor and exposed joints make them easy targets for the clone troopers. Distracting a battle droid is simple given their short attention spans. Battle droids often whine and make bad puns — which make them targets worth blasting.

PARTS PRACTICE

Draw some parts after a
battle droid had a run-in
with a lightsaber.

BATTLE HAZARDS

Battle droids might be easy to destroy, but many tougher weapons are in store for the Jedi.

DROIDEKAS

Droidekas use their powerful twin blasters to attack targets, while protecting themselves with their compact deflector shield generators.

DROIDEKAS

Droidekas use their powerful twin blasters to attack targets, while protecting themselves with their compact deflector shield generators.

SUPER BATTLE DROID

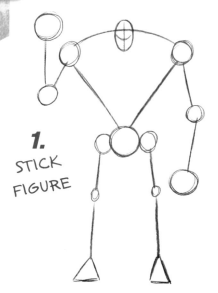

1.
STICK
FIGURE

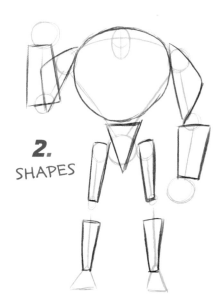

2.
SHAPES

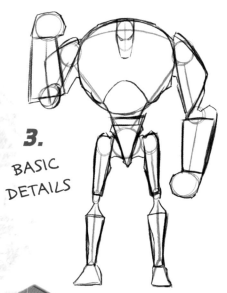

3.
BASIC
DETAILS

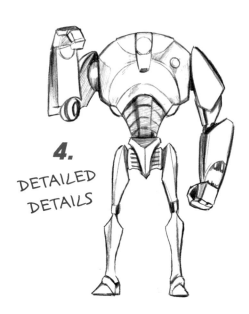

4.
DETAILED
DETAILS

FOLLOW THE STEPS TO DRAW
A SUPER BATTLE DROID.
Here's a sketch to help
you get started.

SUPER BATTLE DROIDS

Larger than battle droids, these bulkier droids have better armor and come equipped with double-laser cannons. They are fearless and relentless in battle situations.

1. STICK FIGURE

2. SHAPES

3. BASIC DETAILS

4. DETAILED DETAILS

FOLLOW THE STEPS TO DRAW A DROIDEKA.
Here's a sketch to
help you get started.

DROIDEKA

MORE

4 STEPS

1.

STICK
FIGURE

2.

SHAPES

3.

BASIC
DETAILS

4.

DETAILED
DETAILS

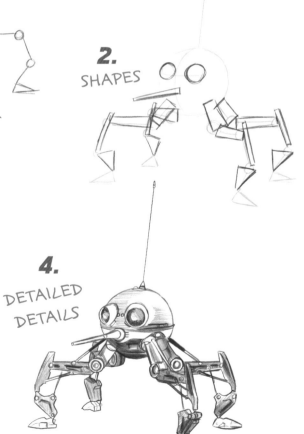

DWARF SPIDER DROID

The four-legged arachnid-like droid marches into battle while shooting a deadly and destructive laser cannon.

FOLLOW THE STEPS TO DRAW A SPIDER DROID. Here's a sketch to help you get started.

DRAW YOUR WEAPON

All lightsabers have a cylindrical shape and basic parts, which include a control button that ignites the blade of pure energy that can deflect blaster bolts and cut through almost anything. Other parts include focusing crystals, lens, power cells, and a handgrip. Because Jedi build their lightsabers from scratch, each hilt is unique.

YOUR TURN

USE ALL THAT YOU HAVE LEARNED TO DRAW THESE LIGHT-SABER HANDLES ON YOUR OWN. Start with a stick figure, then add simple shapes, then the details. One step at a time.

NOW YOU TRY

YODA

The Jedi Master's lightsaber, also called a shoto, is smaller to fit his size and makes swift combat easier.

ANAKIN SKYWALKER

This is one of several lightsabers built by Anakin, who is highly skilled in various forms of combat. The hilt has a solid casing, a ridged handgrip, and emits a blue blade.

ASAJJ VENTRESS

Her two curved lightsaber hilts can connect to form a single saberstaff that she often uses in the Jar'Kai form of combat. Both of her lightsabers have red blades.

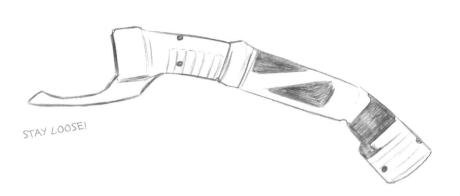

STAY LOOSE!

COUNT DOOKU

The Separatist leader's lightsaber hilt is curved and includes a blade-emitter guard. The shape of the hilt makes overhand strikes more powerful.

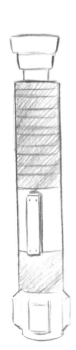

OBI-WAN KENOBI

The Jedi Master specializes in Form III of lightsaber combat which focuses on defensive maneuvers. Obi-Wan's hilt has a ridged handgrip and emits a blue blade.

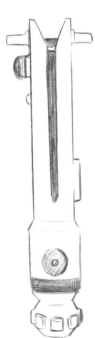

AHSOKA TANO

This strong-willed Padawan uses a sleekly designed lightsaber that emits an emerald blade. She's skilled in the Shien form of lightsaber combat, often using a reverse grip.

FINAL CHALLENGE

TIME TO PUT IT ALL TOGETHER.
On this page we've given you a light blue sketch to trace. Create overlines, study the shapes, and add color if you like.

THEN ON THE OPPOSITE PAGE DRAW R2-D2 AND C-3PO FROM SCRATCH.

NOW YOU!

REMEMBER
1. STICK FIGURES
2. SHAPES
3. BASIC DETAILS
4. DETAILED DETAILS

CREDITS

THANKS

ART DIRECTION \\\\\\\\\\\\\\\ April Chorba
BOOK DESIGN \\\\\\\\\\\\\\\ Martine Cameau
ILLUSTRATIONS \\\\\\\\\\\\\\\\\\ Grant Gould
PHOTOGRAPHY \\\\\\\\\\\\\\\\ Joseph Quever
DEVELOPMENT \\ April Chorba and Michael Sherman
CLONE-TASTIC \\\\\\\\\\\\\\\ Bonnie Burton
FORCEFUL SOURCING \\\\\\\\\\\\ Kelly Shaffer
TRAFFIC CONTROL \\\\\\\\\\\\ Gary Mcdonald
LUCASFILM \\\\\\\\\\\\Troy Alders, Leland Chee, Stacey Cheregotis, Jonathan W. Rinzler, Carol Roeder, and a special thanks to Lucasfilm Animation and Lucasfilm Animation Singapore
HUMAN BATTLE DROID \\\\\\ Michael Sherman
SPECIAL THANKS \\\ Armin Bautista, Hez Chorba, Jenna Nybank, Sam Sherman